This Garden Planner

belongs to -

_____

_____

_____

Annual Rainfall Chart

	JAN	FEB	MAR	APR	MAY	JUNE	JULY	AUG	SEP	OCT	NOV	DEC
1												
2												
3												
4												
5												
6												
7												
8												
9												
10												
11												
12												
13												
14												
15												
16												
17												
18												
19												
20												
21												
22												
23												
24												
25												
26												
27												
28												
29												
30												
31												
TOT												

If you don't have a rain gauge in your garden, consider using colored pencils to color the grids of the rainfall chart to keep track of weather cycles.

Seasonal Planting Chart

Date	Winter			Spring			Summer			Autumn		
Season	Early	Middle	Late	Early	Middle	Late	Early	Middle	Late	Early	Middle	Late

Spring

Spring Garden Planner

Garden Tasks for the month of _____

Weather

Sow	Plant	Harvest	Feed
			Prune

Notes

Month _____

Monday

Tuesday

Wednesday

Thursday

Friday

Saturday

Sunday

To Do
❏
❏
❏
❏
❏
❏
❏
❏
❏
❏
❏
❏
❏
❏
❏
❏
❏
❏
❏
❏
❏
❏
❏
❏

Month _____

Monday

Tuesday

Wednesday

Thursday

Friday

Saturday

Sunday

To Do
❑
❑
❑
❑
❑
❑
❑
❑
❑
❑
❑
❑
❑
❑
❑
❑
❑
❑
❑
❑
❑
❑
❑
❑
❑

Month _____

Monday

Tuesday

Wednesday

Thursday

Friday

Saturday

Sunday

To Do
❑
❑
❑
❑
❑
❑
❑
❑
❑
❑
❑
❑
❑
❑
❑
❑
❑
❑
❑
❑
❑
❑
❑
❑
❑

Month _____

Monday

Tuesday

Wednesday

Thursday

Friday

Saturday

Sunday

To Do
❑
❑
❑
❑
❑
❑
❑
❑
❑
❑
❑
❑
❑
❑
❑
❑
❑
❑
❑
❑
❑
❑
❑
❑

Garden Tasks for the month of _____

Weather

Sow	Plant	Harvest	Feed
			Prune

Notes

Month _____

Monday

Tuesday

Wednesday

Thursday

Friday

Saturday

Sunday

To Do
☐
☐
☐
☐
☐
☐
☐
☐
☐
☐
☐
☐
☐
☐
☐
☐
☐
☐
☐
☐
☐
☐
☐
☐
☐

Month _____

Monday

Tuesday

Wednesday

Thursday

Friday

Saturday

Sunday

To Do
❑
❑
❑
❑
❑
❑
❑
❑
❑
❑
❑
❑
❑
❑
❑
❑
❑
❑
❑
❑
❑
❑
❑
❑

Month

Monday

Tuesday

Wednesday

Thursday

Friday

Saturday

Sunday

To Do
☐
☐
☐
☐
☐
☐
☐
☐
☐
☐
☐
☐
☐
☐
☐
☐
☐
☐
☐
☐
☐
☐
☐
☐

Month _____

Monday

Tuesday

Wednesday

Thursday

Friday

Saturday

Sunday

To Do
❑
❑
❑
❑
❑
❑
❑
❑
❑
❑
❑
❑
❑
❑
❑
❑
❑
❑
❑
❑
❑
❑
❑
❑
❑
❑
❑

Garden Tasks for the month of _____

Weather

_____
_____
_____
_____
_____
_____

Sow	Plant	Harvest	Feed
			Prune

Notes

Month

Monday

Tuesday

Wednesday

Thursday

Friday

Saturday

Sunday

To Do
☐
☐
☐
☐
☐
☐
☐
☐
☐
☐
☐
☐
☐
☐
☐
☐
☐
☐
☐
☐
☐
☐
☐
☐
☐

Month _____

Monday

Tuesday

Wednesday

Thursday

Friday

Saturday

Sunday

To Do
☐
☐
☐
☐
☐
☐
☐
☐
☐
☐
☐
☐
☐
☐
☐
☐
☐
☐
☐
☐
☐
☐
☐
☐

Month

Monday

Tuesday

Wednesday

Thursday

Friday

Saturday

Sunday

To Do

- ☐
- ☐
- ☐
- ☐
- ☐
- ☐
- ☐
- ☐
- ☐
- ☐
- ☐
- ☐
- ☐
- ☐
- ☐
- ☐
- ☐
- ☐
- ☐
- ☐
- ☐
- ☐
- ☐
- ☐
- ☐
- ☐

Month _____

Monday

Tuesday

Wednesday

Thursday

Friday

Saturday

Sunday

To Do
❑
❑
❑
❑
❑
❑
❑
❑
❑
❑
❑
❑
❑
❑
❑
❑
❑
❑
❑
❑
❑
❑
❑
❑
❑

Month _____

Monday

Tuesday

Wednesday

Thursday

Friday

Saturday

Sunday

To Do
☐ _____
☐ _____
☐ _____
☐ _____
☐ _____
☐ _____
☐ _____
☐ _____
☐ _____
☐ _____
☐ _____
☐ _____
☐ _____
☐ _____
☐ _____
☐ _____
☐ _____
☐ _____
☐ _____
☐ _____
☐ _____
☐ _____
☐ _____
☐ _____
☐ _____

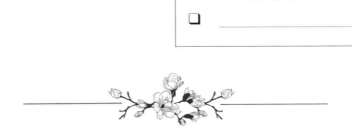

Notes

Summer Garden Planner

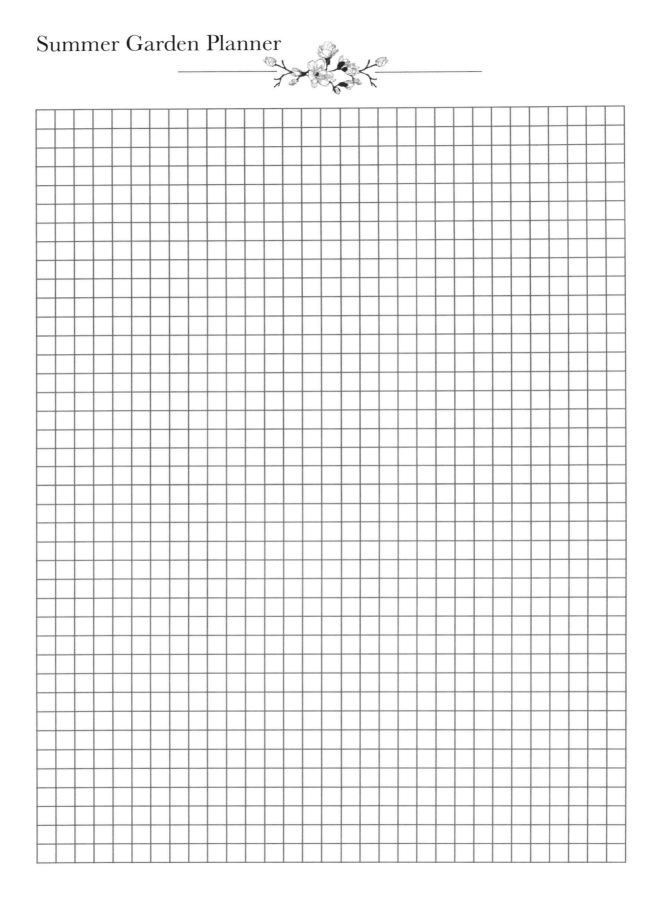

Garden Tasks for the month of _____

Weather

Sow	Plant	Harvest	Feed
			Prune

Month _____

Monday

Tuesday

Wednesday

Thursday

Friday

Saturday

Sunday

To Do
❑
❑
❑
❑
❑
❑
❑
❑
❑
❑
❑
❑
❑
❑
❑
❑
❑
❑
❑
❑
❑
❑
❑
❑

Month _____

Monday

Tuesday

Wednesday

Thursday

Friday

Saturday

Sunday

To Do
❑
❑
❑
❑
❑
❑
❑
❑
❑
❑
❑
❑
❑
❑
❑
❑
❑
❑
❑
❑
❑
❑
❑
❑
❑

Month _____

Monday

Tuesday

Wednesday

Thursday

Friday

Saturday

Sunday

To Do
❑
❑
❑
❑
❑
❑
❑
❑
❑
❑
❑
❑
❑
❑
❑
❑
❑
❑
❑
❑
❑
❑
❑
❑
❑
❑

Month

Monday

Tuesday

Wednesday

Thursday

Friday

Saturday

Sunday

To Do

- ❏
- ❏
- ❏
- ❏
- ❏
- ❏
- ❏
- ❏
- ❏
- ❏
- ❏
- ❏
- ❏
- ❏
- ❏
- ❏
- ❏
- ❏
- ❏
- ❏
- ❏
- ❏
- ❏
- ❏
- ❏
- ❏

Garden Tasks for the month of _____

Weather

Sow	Plant	Harvest	Feed
			Prune

Notes

Month _____

Monday

Tuesday

Wednesday

Thursday

Friday

Saturday

Sunday

To Do
❑
❑
❑
❑
❑
❑
❑
❑
❑
❑
❑
❑
❑
❑
❑
❑
❑
❑
❑
❑
❑
❑
❑

Month

Monday

Tuesday

Wednesday

Thursday

Friday

Saturday

Sunday

To Do

- ❏
- ❏
- ❏
- ❏
- ❏
- ❏
- ❏
- ❏
- ❏
- ❏
- ❏
- ❏
- ❏
- ❏
- ❏
- ❏
- ❏
- ❏
- ❏
- ❏
- ❏
- ❏
- ❏
- ❏
- ❏

Month _____

Monday

Tuesday

Wednesday

Thursday

Friday

Saturday

Sunday

To Do
❑ ....
❑ ....
❑ ....
❑ ....
❑ ....
❑ ....
❑ ....
❑ ....
❑ ....
❑ ....
❑ ....
❑ ....
❑ ....
❑ ....
❑ ....
❑ ....
❑ ....
❑ ....
❑ ....
❑ ....
❑ ....
❑ ....
❑ ....

Month _____

Monday

Tuesday

Wednesday

Thursday

Friday

Saturday

Sunday

To Do
❑
❑
❑
❑
❑
❑
❑
❑
❑
❑
❑
❑
❑
❑
❑
❑
❑
❑
❑
❑
❑
❑
❑
❑
❑
❑
❑

Garden Tasks for the month of _____

Weather

Sow	Plant	Harvest	Feed
			Prune

Notes

Month _____

Monday

Tuesday

Wednesday

Thursday

Friday

Saturday

Sunday

To Do

- ❏ _____
- ❏ _____
- ❏ _____
- ❏ _____
- ❏ _____
- ❏ _____
- ❏ _____
- ❏ _____
- ❏ _____
- ❏ _____
- ❏ _____
- ❏ _____
- ❏ _____
- ❏ _____
- ❏ _____
- ❏ _____
- ❏ _____
- ❏ _____
- ❏ _____
- ❏ _____
- ❏ _____
- ❏ _____
- ❏ _____
- ❏ _____
- ❏ _____
- ❏ _____

Month

Monday

Tuesday

Wednesday

Thursday

Friday

Saturday

Sunday

To Do
❑
❑
❑
❑
❑
❑
❑
❑
❑
❑
❑
❑
❑
❑
❑
❑
❑
❑
❑
❑
❑
❑
❑
❑
❑

Month _____

Monday

Tuesday

Wednesday

Thursday

Friday

Saturday

Sunday

To Do
❑
❑
❑
❑
❑
❑
❑
❑
❑
❑
❑
❑
❑
❑
❑
❑
❑
❑
❑
❑
❑
❑
❑
❑

Month

Monday

Tuesday

Wednesday

Thursday

Friday

Saturday

Sunday

To Do
❏
❏
❏
❏
❏
❏
❏
❏
❏
❏
❏
❏
❏
❏
❏
❏
❏
❏
❏
❏
❏
❏
❏
❏

Month _____

Monday

Tuesday

Wednesday

Thursday

Friday

Saturday

Sunday

To Do
☐
☐
☐
☐
☐
☐
☐
☐
☐
☐
☐
☐
☐
☐
☐
☐
☐
☐
☐
☐
☐
☐
☐
☐
☐

Notes

Autumn Garden Planner

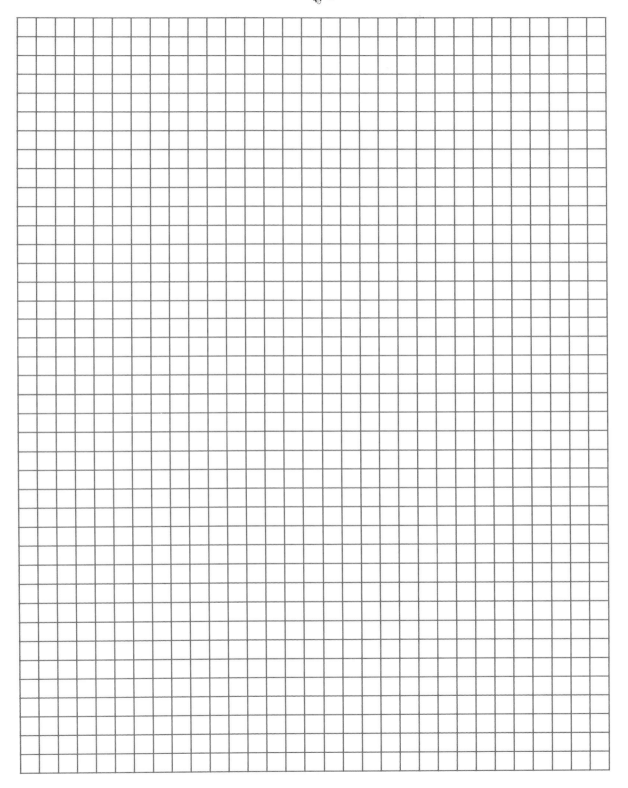

Garden Tasks for the month of _____

Weather

_____
_____
_____
_____
_____
_____
_____
_____

Sow	Plant	Harvest	Feed
			Prune

Month _____

Monday

Tuesday

Wednesday

Thursday

Friday

Saturday

Sunday

To Do
❏ ....
❏ ....
❏ ....
❏ ....
❏ ....
❏ ....
❏ ....
❏ ....
❏ ....
❏ ....
❏ ....
❏ ....
❏ ....
❏ ....
❏ ....
❏ ....
❏ ....
❏ ....
❏ ....
❏ ....
❏ ....
❏ ....
❏ ....
❏ ....
❏ ....

Month _____

Monday

Tuesday

Wednesday

Thursday

Friday

Saturday

Sunday

To Do
❏
❏
❏
❏
❏
❏
❏
❏
❏
❏
❏
❏
❏
❏
❏
❏
❏
❏
❏
❏
❏
❏
❏
❏

Month _____

Monday

Tuesday

Wednesday

Thursday

Friday

Saturday

Sunday

To Do
❑
❑
❑
❑
❑
❑
❑
❑
❑
❑
❑
❑
❑
❑
❑
❑
❑
❑
❑
❑
❑
❑
❑
❑

Month _____

Monday

Tuesday

Wednesday

Thursday

Friday

Saturday

Sunday

To Do
❏
❏
❏
❏
❏
❏
❏
❏
❏
❏
❏
❏
❏
❏
❏
❏
❏
❏
❏
❏
❏
❏
❏
❏
❏

Garden Tasks for the month of _____

Weather

_____
_____
_____
_____
_____
_____
_____
_____

Sow	Plant	Harvest	Feed
			Prune

Notes

Month _____

Monday

Tuesday

Wednesday

Thursday

Friday

Saturday

Sunday

To Do
❑
❑
❑
❑
❑
❑
❑
❑
❑
❑
❑
❑
❑
❑
❑
❑
❑
❑
❑
❑
❑
❑
❑
❑

Month _____

Monday

Tuesday

Wednesday

Thursday

Friday

Saturday

Sunday

To Do
☐
☐
☐
☐
☐
☐
☐
☐
☐
☐
☐
☐
☐
☐
☐
☐
☐
☐
☐
☐
☐
☐
☐
☐
☐

Month _____

Monday

Tuesday

Wednesday

Thursday

Friday

Saturday

Sunday

To Do
❑
❑
❑
❑
❑
❑
❑
❑
❑
❑
❑
❑
❑
❑
❑
❑
❑
❑
❑
❑
❑
❑
❑
❑

Month _____

Monday

Tuesday

Wednesday

Thursday

Friday

Saturday

Sunday

To Do
❏
❏
❏
❏
❏
❏
❏
❏
❏
❏
❏
❏
❏
❏
❏
❏
❏
❏
❏
❏
❏
❏
❏
❏
❏

Garden Tasks for the month of _____

Weather

Sow	Plant	Harvest	Feed
			Prune

Notes

Month _____

Monday

Tuesday

Wednesday

Thursday

Friday

Saturday

Sunday

To Do
❑
❑
❑
❑
❑
❑
❑
❑
❑
❑
❑
❑
❑
❑
❑
❑
❑
❑
❑
❑
❑
❑
❑
❑
❑

Month _____

Monday

Tuesday

Wednesday

Thursday

Friday

Saturday

Sunday

To Do
☐
☐
☐
☐
☐
☐
☐
☐
☐
☐
☐
☐
☐
☐
☐
☐
☐
☐
☐
☐
☐
☐
☐
☐
☐

Month _____

Monday

Tuesday

Wednesday

Thursday

Friday

Saturday

Sunday

To Do
❏
❏
❏
❏
❏
❏
❏
❏
❏
❏
❏
❏
❏
❏
❏
❏
❏
❏
❏
❏
❏
❏
❏
❏

Month _____

Monday

Tuesday

Wednesday

Thursday

Friday

Saturday

Sunday

To Do

- ☐ ....
- ☐ ....
- ☐ ....
- ☐ ....
- ☐ ....
- ☐ ....
- ☐ ....
- ☐ ....
- ☐ ....
- ☐ ....
- ☐ ....
- ☐ ....
- ☐ ....
- ☐ ....
- ☐ ....
- ☐ ....
- ☐ ....
- ☐ ....
- ☐ ....
- ☐ ....
- ☐ ....
- ☐ ....
- ☐ ....
- ☐ ....
- ☐ ....

Month _____

Monday

Tuesday

Wednesday

Thursday

Friday

Saturday

Sunday

To Do
❏
❏
❏
❏
❏
❏
❏
❏
❏
❏
❏
❏
❏
❏
❏
❏
❏
❏
❏
❏
❏
❏
❏
❏
❏

Notes

Winter Garden Planner

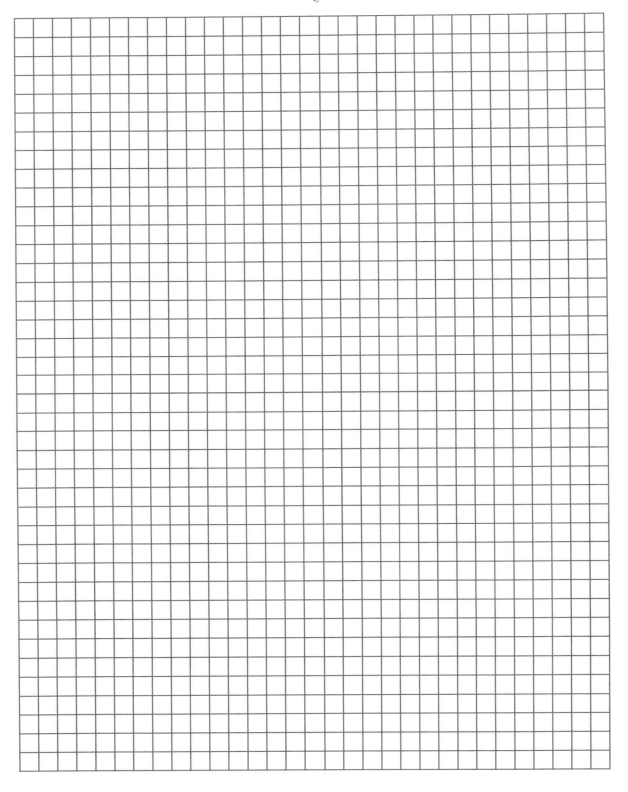

Garden Tasks for the month of _____

Weather

Sow	Plant	Harvest	Feed
			Prune

Month

Monday

Tuesday

Wednesday

Thursday

Friday

Saturday

Sunday

To Do

- ❑ ....
- ❑ ....
- ❑ ....
- ❑ ....
- ❑ ....
- ❑ ....
- ❑ ....
- ❑ ....
- ❑ ....
- ❑ ....
- ❑ ....
- ❑ ....
- ❑ ....
- ❑ ....
- ❑ ....
- ❑ ....
- ❑ ....
- ❑ ....
- ❑ ....
- ❑ ....
- ❑ ....
- ❑ ....
- ❑ ....
- ❑ ....
- ❑ ....

Month

Monday

Tuesday

Wednesday

Thursday

Friday

Saturday

Sunday

To Do
❏
❏
❏
❏
❏
❏
❏
❏
❏
❏
❏
❏
❏
❏
❏
❏
❏
❏
❏
❏
❏
❏
❏
❏

Month _____

Monday

Tuesday

Wednesday

Thursday

Friday

Saturday

Sunday

To Do
☐
☐
☐
☐
☐
☐
☐
☐
☐
☐
☐
☐
☐
☐
☐
☐
☐
☐
☐
☐
☐
☐
☐
☐
☐

Month _____

Monday

Tuesday

Wednesday

Thursday

Friday

Saturday

Sunday

To Do
❑ _____
❑ _____
❑ _____
❑ _____
❑ _____
❑ _____
❑ _____
❑ _____
❑ _____
❑ _____
❑ _____
❑ _____
❑ _____
❑ _____
❑ _____
❑ _____
❑ _____
❑ _____
❑ _____
❑ _____
❑ _____
❑ _____
❑ _____
❑ _____
❑ _____

Garden Tasks for the month of _____

Weather

_____
_____
_____
_____
_____
_____
_____

Sow	Plant	Harvest	Feed
			Prune

Notes

Month _____

Monday

Tuesday

Wednesday

Thursday

Friday

Saturday

Sunday

To Do
❑ _____
❑ _____
❑ _____
❑ _____
❑ _____
❑ _____
❑ _____
❑ _____
❑ _____
❑ _____
❑ _____
❑ _____
❑ _____
❑ _____
❑ _____
❑ _____
❑ _____
❑ _____
❑ _____
❑ _____
❑ _____
❑ _____
❑ _____
❑ _____
❑ _____
❑ _____

Month _____

Monday

Tuesday

Wednesday

Thursday

Friday

Saturday

Sunday

To Do
❑
❑
❑
❑
❑
❑
❑
❑
❑
❑
❑
❑
❑
❑
❑
❑
❑
❑
❑
❑
❑
❑
❑
❑
❑
❑

Month _____

Monday

Tuesday

Wednesday

Thursday

Friday

Saturday

Sunday

To Do
❑ ....
❑ ....
❑ ....
❑ ....
❑ ....
❑ ....
❑ ....
❑ ....
❑ ....
❑ ....
❑ ....
❑ ....
❑ ....
❑ ....
❑ ....
❑ ....
❑ ....
❑ ....
❑ ....
❑ ....
❑ ....
❑ ....
❑ ....
❑ ....
❑ ....
❑ ....

Month _____

Monday

Tuesday

Wednesday

Thursday

Friday

Saturday

Sunday

To Do
❑
❑
❑
❑
❑
❑
❑
❑
❑
❑
❑
❑
❑
❑
❑
❑
❑
❑
❑
❑
❑
❑
❑
❑

Garden Tasks for the month of _____

Sow	Plant	Harvest	Feed
			Prune

Notes

Month _____

Monday

Tuesday

Wednesday

Thursday

Friday

Saturday

Sunday

To Do
❑ _____
❑ _____
❑ _____
❑ _____
❑ _____
❑ _____
❑ _____
❑ _____
❑ _____
❑ _____
❑ _____
❑ _____
❑ _____
❑ _____
❑ _____
❑ _____
❑ _____
❑ _____
❑ _____
❑ _____
❑ _____
❑ _____
❑ _____
❑ _____
❑ _____
❑ _____

Month _____

Monday

Tuesday

Wednesday

Thursday

Friday

Saturday

Sunday

To Do
❑ ....
❑ ....
❑ ....
❑ ....
❑ ....
❑ ....
❑ ....
❑ ....
❑ ....
❑ ....
❑ ....
❑ ....
❑ ....
❑ ....
❑ ....
❑ ....
❑ ....
❑ ....
❑ ....
❑ ....
❑ ....
❑ ....
❑ ....
❑ ....

Month _____

Monday

Tuesday

Wednesday

Thursday

Friday

Saturday

Sunday

To Do
☐
☐
☐
☐
☐
☐
☐
☐
☐
☐
☐
☐
☐
☐
☐
☐
☐
☐
☐
☐
☐
☐
☐
☐
☐
☐

Month

Monday

Tuesday

Wednesday

Thursday

Friday

Saturday

Sunday

To Do
☐
☐
☐
☐
☐
☐
☐
☐
☐
☐
☐
☐
☐
☐
☐
☐
☐
☐
☐
☐
☐
☐
☐
☐
☐
☐

Month _____

Monday

Tuesday

Wednesday

Thursday

Friday

Saturday

Sunday

To Do

- ❏ _____
- ❏ _____
- ❏ _____
- ❏ _____
- ❏ _____
- ❏ _____
- ❏ _____
- ❏ _____
- ❏ _____
- ❏ _____
- ❏ _____
- ❏ _____
- ❏ _____
- ❏ _____
- ❏ _____
- ❏ _____
- ❏ _____
- ❏ _____
- ❏ _____
- ❏ _____
- ❏ _____
- ❏ _____
- ❏ _____
- ❏ _____
- ❏ _____

Notes

Flowers

Plant	Date Planted	Expected Bloom	Observations and Notes

Herbs and Vegetables

Vegetable/Herb	Date Planted	Yield	Observations and Notes

Potted Plants

Plant	Date Planted	Expected Bloom	Observations and Notes

Pests and Diseases

Date	Pest/Disease ID	Problem	Treatment	Observations and Notes

Harvest Tracker

Plant	Date	Quantity/Yield	Observations and Notes

Notes

Printed in Great
Britain
by Amazon